How to drink wine out of fish heads while cooking lobster in a Volkswagen hub cap

Easy Seafood Recipes

Many fish together
are known as a school.
Clearly this is not a school

LAGOON BOOKS

Published in 2000 by Lagoon Books
PO Box 311, KT2 5QW, UK
PO Box 990676, Boston, MA 02199, USA
WWW.LAGOONGAMES.COM

LAGOON WOMAN TESTED

ISBN: 1902813138

First published in Australia in 1998 by
Pan Macmillan Australia Pty Limited

Copyright © 1998 Billy Blue Merchandising Pty Ltd

Recipes by Helen Tracey and Linda Kaplan

Additional writing by Ross Renwick

Supervising Chefs Matt Blundell and Gavin Cummins
of Kentra Double Bay Australia

Managing Director Aaron Kaplan Creative Director Ross Renwick

Printed in Singapore

mashed potato is now an illegal substance

9	**LONELY ISLANDS** GRILLED LOBSTER TAILS
12	**MALIBU DREAMING** WHITING IN LIME AND PASSIONFRUIT SAUCE
14	**SLOW WHITE CLOUD** FISH STOCK
15	**SONG OF SIAM** SPICY THAI FISH SOUP
16	**BONDI MOON** SMOKED OYSTER SOUP
17	**PEPPERCORN SUNRISE** MUSSELS WITH FENNEL
18	**RIVER TREE** SHELLFISH AND AVOCADO SOUP
19	**BLUE RAIN FALLING** FISH SANDWICH
20	**MOON SEA MAN WOMAN** COD CHOWDER
22	**KOSCIUSZKO WITH ORANGE SKY** PRAWN MYSTERY
24	**GREEN FISH JUMPING** WARM BALSAMIC FISH SALAD
26	**PINK SEA RISING** FISH STEW
27	**CYCLONE ERNIE** FISH PARCELS
30	**WARM DARWIN DAYS** TANGY FISH FILLETS
31	**BLUE PACIFIC NOON** GRILLED ATLANTIC SALMON CUTLETS
32	**BUTTERNUT BLUE** CRISP PRAWN SALAD
34	**MANGO MANGO** SMOKED SALMON, AVOCADO AND MANGO SALAD
36	**FREE CHILLI** STEAMED FISH
38	**CHINATOWN CUTLETS** ORIENTAL TUNA
39	**PRINCESS'S TAKEAWAY** SALMON AND CAVIAR PIZZA
42	**THURSDAY'S BREAKFAST** STEAMED CRAB
44	**WARATAH STREET HIDEOUT** TUNA AND SPAGHETTI
45	**MANGO WATERFALL** REDFISH WITH MANGO
46	**RED BUTTERFLY** MUSTARD PRAWNS
48	**COOK IT AGAIN SAM** MOROCCAN FISH
50	**JAMAICA RAFT** CREOLE FILLETS

51 **JAILHOUSE FILLET** DORY FILLETS WITH AVOCADO MACADAMIA CREAM

52 **SLARKI YARKI** TERIYAKI KINGFISH

53 **ET TU BANANA** BANANA OR MANGO FILLETS

54 **YELLOW BUTTERFLY** PASTA WITH SALMON

55 **SOUGHING SEA** CEVICHE

56 **COOKING FISH** POACHING, BAKING, PAN FRYING, STEAMING, GRILLING, BARBECUING

60 **FISH AND CRUSTACEAN IDENTIFICATION**

Buying the Best Fish.
What to look for:

A nice even personality

Independent income

Normal sexual habits
(or other if preferred)

Avoid fish that have been written on

Also look for:

Bright eyes which protrude

Clean, fresh smell

Bright spots and marking

Firm fins

Shiny scales

Nice smile

ET TU FLATHEAD

Lures are objects which you put on your fishing line instead of bait.

They are deceptively designed to make fish think that it's regular food.

Lures come in pressure-packed cards with optimistic advertising copy.

However, I'm here to tell you that the fish don't believe the copy.

When you decide to use lures instead of bait you're already on the way to a better life.

Why? Because you don't have to fool around with dirty, stinking bait.

Put the lure on your fishing line and cast it into promising waters. (For a definition of promising waters refer to other sources.)

The whole affair works better if you cast the lure and then drink a small glass of very fine English sherry as you pull it in.

How, you may ask, can I drink a glass of sherry while holding the rod with one hand and winding in the lure with the other? Easy, I answer. By making a structure from a metal

COATHANGER THAT FITS AROUND YOUR HEAD AND HOLDS A SHERRY GLASS TO YOUR LIPS.

I HAVE BEEN FISHING WITH LURES FOR FIFTEEN YEARS AND HAVE NEVER CAUGHT A SINGLE FISH. I HAVEN'T EVEN HAD A BITE. BUT I HAVE DRUNK SOME VERY FINE SHERRY AND SPENT MANY BEAUTIFUL AFTERNOONS OUTDOORS.

SO THE MAIN ADVANTAGE OF LURE FISHING IS THAT YOU PROBABLY WON'T HAVE ANY DEALINGS WITH LIVE FISH. WITHIN REASON I CAN GUARANTEE IT.

I HAVE NOW TOLD YOU HOW TO HAVE A PERFECT FISHING LIFE. WITHOUT BAIT. WITHOUT FISH. WITH SHERRY. OR THE CORDIAL OF YOUR CHOICE.

THERE IS ONLY ONE RULE. BUY WHAT YOU NEED FROM THE FISH SHOP.

UNEXPLAINED DOG

Unexplained tree
(unexplained
cowgirls
may occur)

LONELY ISLANDS GRILLED LOBSTER TAILS

SERVES 4.

I want to tell you about my attitude to drinking.

It isn't really an attitude. It's just one of the things that happens beyond my control.

In the introduction speech to this small volume called Et Tu Flathead, I mentioned a structure made from a wire coathanger that holds a glass of fine English sherry to your lips.

I expect by now you have made one and have discovered that the use of foam rubber makes the grip on your head and on the sherry glass a little easier.

And you may have also discovered that it's quite a handy structure as it leaves both hands free to get on with life's work.

Forgive me, but you have probably also discovered how difficult it is to refill a glass that is so close to your chin unless you are extraordinarily short-sighted.

I am working on a refilling device, something like a medical drip that is attached to a crane-like structure which in turn is attached to the sherry glass rig.

It is a less than minimalist solution so while I simplify it, do the best you can with the rig you have.

I WAS ABOUT TO TELL YOU ABOUT MY ATTITUDE TO DRINKING. I DON'T DRINK OFTEN. BUT WHEN I COOK I DRINK.

SOME SAY THIS IS UNJUSTIFIABLY DANGEROUS BUT IT'S NOT AS DANGEROUS AS DRIVING A TRAIN WHEN DRINKING...OR DECIDING YOU MIGHT LIKE TO GET MARRIED WHILE DRINKING.

I DON'T QUITE KNOW WHERE I'M GOING WITH THIS. FOR EXAMPLE, WHEN I'M COOKING MALIBU DREAMING, IT IS TWO GLASSES OF A NICE LITTLE CHARDONNAY FROM AUSTRALIA CALLED POET'S PILES AT ABOUT $2.300 A BOTTLE.

COOK IT AGAIN SAM IS TWO GLASSES OF A WHITE RUM MIXED WITH COCONUT MILK AND LIMES. A NASTY LITTLE DRINK INDEED.

I PRESENT TO YOU LONELY ISLANDS GRILLED LOBSTER TAILS. I WOULD THINK THAT THE COOKING TIME IS ABOUT THREE GLASSES OF A NICE CANARY FROM THE SOUTH-EAST CORNER OF SPAIN.

4 GREEN LOBSTER TAILS

125ml/$^1/_2$ CUP MELTED BUTTER

3 TABLESPOONS LEMON JUICE

SALT AND PEPPER

CHOPPED PARSLEY

CHOPPED GARLIC

SLIT UNDERSIDE OF LOBSTER TAILS ONCE OR TWICE WITH A SHARP KNIFE.

PLACE UNDER GRILL, SHELL SIDE UP.

COOK UNTIL RED.

TURN OVER, RETURN TO GRILL, BASTING OFTEN WITH LEMON JUICE, MELTED BUTTER AND GARLIC.

COOK UNTIL MEAT IS TENDER AND WHITE.

SEASON WITH SALT, PEPPER AND PARSLEY.

VARIATION: HEAT OVEN TO 180°C/350°F/ GAS MARK 4
PUT TAILS ON OVEN TRAY, BAKE 15-20 MINUTES, DEPENDING ON SIZE. SQUEEZE LEMON JUICE OVER AND SPRINKLE WITH PEPPER.

SUCCESSFUL FISH SHOP

MALIBU DREAMING WHITING IN LIME AND PASSIONFRUIT SAUCE

SERVES 4.

I live in a place which has a beach and a port and a modicum of charm but not much chance of a great cappuccino.

At the north end of the beach there's a nice surfing wave when the nor'-easters begin blowing in spring. The wave runs across a reef of boulders edged by bright green seagrass, and if you're cruising through that little picture on your malibu surfboard you eventually run onto a sand bottom.

And there you see them, or at least you see their shadows because their bodies are so transparent...the new season's whiting. One of the world's great eating fish.

But if you're not cruising through the clear bright green spring water at Avalon on your elegant surfboard, you can see them at the fish shop.

MYSTERY SURFBOARD

500g/1lb WHITING FILLETS

60ml/¼ CUP VERMOUTH

80ml/⅓ CUP FRESH LIME JUICE

5 TABLESPOONS FRESH PASSIONFRUIT PULP

¼ TEASPOON SUGAR

SALT

POUR VERMOUTH AND JUICE OVER FISH AND SIMMER UNTIL FLESH FLAKES.

REMOVE TO WARM PLATTER AND KEEP WARM.

TO PAN JUICES, ADD PASSIONFRUIT PULP, SUGAR AND SALT TO TASTE.

HEAT SAUCE UNTIL HOT.

POUR OVER FISH AND SERVE.

SLOW WHITE CLOUD FISH STOCK

**3 FISH SKELETONS, INCLUDING SCALED
FISH HEADS AND TRIMMINGS AND
PRAWN SHELLS, ETC (IF THAT'S TOO
TECHNICAL, THROW IN A COUPLE OF
FISH CUTLETS OR SMALL SCALED FISH)**

**WATER, 1 TEASPOON SALT, 1 BAY LEAF,
2 SLICES LEMON, 1 STICK OF CELERY,
1 ONION, CHOPPED, 1 CARROT,
CHOPPED, SPRIG OF PARSLEY,
3 BLACK PEPPERCORNS**

WASH FISH PIECES THOROUGHLY.

PUT IN HEAVY SAUCEPAN.

ADD SALT, PEPPERCORNS, LEMON, BAY LEAF, WATER
AND VEGETABLES.

BRING TO BOIL AND SIMMER APPROXIMATELY 1 HOUR.

STRAIN STOCK CAREFULLY THROUGH A FINE STRAINER.

WHEN COLD, REFRIGERATE.

KEEPS FOR TWO DAYS, FREEZE IF NEEDED LATER.

SONG OF SIAM SPICY THAI FISH SOUP

SERVES 4.

- **1 LITRE/1³/₄ PINTS CLEAR CHICKEN STOCK (FROM THE DELI)**
- **1 TABLESPOON THAI FISH SAUCE**
- **2 TABLESPOONS FRESH LIME OR LEMON JUICE**
- **5 STALKS LEMON GRASS**
- **1¹/₂ TEASPOONS RED CURRY PASTE**
- **400g/14oz MIXED FRESH FISH, CUBED**
- **8 FRESH PRAWNS, PEELED AND DEVEINED**
- **12 BUTTON MUSHROOMS**
- **FRESH CORIANDER, CHOPPED**
- **4 FRESH CHILLIES, SEEDED AND SLICED**

BRING STOCK TO BOIL.

ADD FISH SAUCE, LIME OR LEMON JUICE, LEMON GRASS, CURRY PASTE AND CHILLIES.

BRING TO BOIL.

TASTE FOR SPICINESS.

ADD FISH, PRAWNS AND MUSHROOMS.

SIMMER UNTIL FISH IS COOKED.

REMOVE LEMON GRASS.

SERVE SPRINKLED WITH CORIANDER.

BONDI MOON SMOKED OYSTER SOUP

SERVES 4.

2 DESSERTSPOONS BUTTER

35g/¹/₄ CUP PLAIN FLOUR

**750ml/3 CUPS FISH STOCK
  (YOU COULD USE WATER)**

250ml/1 CUP MILK

**1 OR 2 CANS SMOKED OYSTERS,
  DRAINED AND CHOPPED**

PINCH GROUND NUTMEG

SALT AND PEPPER

1 TEASPOON ANCHOVY SAUCE

¹/₄ TEASPOON LEMON JUICE

CHOPPED PARSLEY OR CHIVES

SOUR CREAM (OPTIONAL)

MELT BUTTER IN SAUCEPAN.

STIR IN FLOUR AND COOK, STIRRING CONSTANTLY,
UNTIL FROTHY.

GRADUALLY ADD STOCK AND MILK, STILL
STIRRING CONSTANTLY.

COOK 5 MINUTES, UNTIL MIXTURE THICKENS.

SEASON WITH SALT, PEPPER AND NUTMEG TO TASTE.

STIR IN OYSTERS, LEMON JUICE AND ANCHOVY SAUCE.

SERVE GARNISHED WITH PARSLEY OR CHIVES AND
PERHAPS A DOLLOP OF SOUR CREAM.

PEPPERCORN SUNRISE MUSSELS WITH FENNEL

SERVES 4-6.

3kg/6$^1/_2$lb MUSSELS
375ml/1$^1/_2$ CUPS CLARET
2 CLOVES GARLIC, CUT IN HALF
SEVERAL PARSLEY SPRIGS
$^1/_2$ TEASPOON BLACK PEPPERCORNS
SALT TO TASTE
1 HEAD OF FENNEL, FINELY CHOPPED
3 SPRING ONIONS, CHOPPED
2 BAY LEAVES
10 BASIL LEAVES, TORN

BRING EVERYTHING EXCEPT MUSSELS TO BOIL IN LARGE SAUCEPAN.

SCRUB MUSSELS AND REMOVE BEARDS.

ADD AS MANY AS YOU CAN TO SAUCEPAN AND COOK UNTIL OPEN.

REMOVE, THEN COOK REMAINDER.

DISCARD ANY UNOPENED SHELLS (THEY MAY BE BAD).

SERVE SHELLS IN GENEROUS-SIZED BOWLS WITH STRAINED STOCK POURED OVER THEM.

RIVER TREE SHELLFISH AND AVOCADO SOUP

SERVES 4.

1 TABLESPOON MELTED BUTTER
2 RIPE AVOCADOS
500ml/2 CUPS CHICKEN STOCK,
  OR 1 STOCK CUBE AND WATER
500ml/1 CUP CREAM (OR $\frac{1}{2}$ CREAM
AND MILK)
2 TABLESPOONS SHERRY
SALT AND PEPPER
ABOUT 350g/12oz COOKED SHELLFISH —
  SCALLOPS, MUSSELS, CLAMS,
  CRABMEAT. INCLUDE PRAWNS
  IF DESIRED

IN BLENDER, COMBINE ALL INGREDIENTS
EXCEPT SHELLFISH.

BLEND UNTIL AVOCADO IS CREAMY.

PEEL AND DEVEIN PRAWNS. LEAVE CLAMS
AND MUSSELS IN SHELL.

ADD SHELLFISH TO AVOCADO MIXTURE.

HEAT GRADUALLY, STIRRING CONSTANTLY.

SERVE HOT OR COLD.

BLUE RAIN FALLING FISH SANDWICH

SERVES 4.

2 STICKS CRISP CELERY, FINELY CHOPPED
1 TABLESPOON MAYONNAISE
PINCH OF PAPRIKA
1 TEASPOON CHOPPED BASIL
1 TEASPOON CHOPPED DILL
**450g/2 CUPS COOKED,
  BONED, FLAKED FISH**
SALT AND PEPPER
**SMALL FRENCH LOAF, SLICED
  HORIZONTALLY AND BUTTERED**

COMBINE CELERY, MAYONNAISE, PAPRIKA, BASIL, DILL,
FISH, SALT AND PEPPER IN BLENDER (OR MIX WELL IN
BASIN OR JAR).

SPREAD MIXTURE ON BREAD HALVES AND
JOIN TOGETHER.

CAN BE WARMED IN OVEN BEFORE SERVING.

GOOD AT A PICNIC OR FOR A WEEKEND LUNCH.

MOON SEA MAN WOMAN

COD CHOWDER

SERVES 4-6.

125g/4oz BACON, DICED

1 MEDIUM ONION, CHOPPED

$^1/_2$ CAPSICUM, FINELY CHOPPED

450g/1lb FILLET OF COD

310ml/1 $^1/_4$ CUP FISH STOCK (OPTIONAL)

2 MEDIUM POTATOES, DICED

BLACK PEPPER

500ml/$^3/_4$ – 1 PINT MILK

PAPRIKA, CHIVES OR PARSLEY FOR GARNISH

1 DESSERTSPOON TURMERIC (OPTIONAL)

SAUTE BACON AND ONION IN MEDIUM SAUCEPAN UNTIL BACON IS CRISP.

REMOVE BONES AND SCALES FROM COD AND SIMMER 10 MINUTES IN FISH STOCK (OR LIGHTLY SALTED WATER).

STIR IN COD (IN BITE-SIZE PIECES), LIQUID, POTATOES, CAPSICUM, PEPPER AND BACON/ONION MIXTURE.

BRING TO BOIL.

COVER AND SIMMER UNTIL POTATOES ARE TENDER.

STIR IN MILK THEN HEAT, STIRRING OCCASIONALLY, UNTIL HOT.

DO NOT BOIL.

GARNISH WITH PAPRIKA, CHIVES OR PARSLEY.

ADD TURMERIC.

SERVE WITH CRUSTY BREAD.

FISHING CAN BE FUN

KOSCIUSZKO WITH ORANGE SKY

PRAWN MYSTERY

SERVES 4.

It's OK for you cruising through this little cookbook. You can put it down when you like.

I'm the one who has to do the bloody writing. Sitting here, nothing to eat, and I've named this bloody recipe Kosciuszko with Orange Sky. And it's a prawn recipe.

But the editor's a snivelling drunk...he probably won't even notice this unmitigated crap. So if you're reading this, he hasn't.

½ TEASPOON CHOPPED DILL

4 SLICES BREAD, BUTTERED

50g/2oz EMMENTHAL CHEESE, GRATED

3 DESSERTSPOONS CREAM

3 TABLESPOONS MAYONNAISE

250g/9oz SMALL PRAWNS, COOKED AND PEELED

4 EGG WHITES, STIFFLY BEATEN

SALT AND PEPPER

PLACE BREAD, BUTTERED SIDE DOWN, ON BAKING TRAY.

COMBINE CHEESE, CREAM, DILL AND MAYONNAISE IN A BOWL.

SEASON.

ADD PRAWNS, RESERVING A FEW FOR GARNISH.

SPREAD MIXTURE ON TOP OF BREAD.

TOP WITH STIFFLY BEATEN EGG WHITES.

BAKE IN PREHEATED OVEN AT 220°C/425°F/GAS MARK 7 UNTIL WELL RISEN AND BROWNED — ABOUT 10-15 MINUTES.

SERVE IMMEDIATELY AS AN EASY LUNCH OR A SPECTACULAR BREAKFAST.

GREEN FISH JUMPING

WARM BALSAMIC FISH SALAD

SERVES 4.

2 TEASPOONS OLIVE OIL

**500g/1lb TUNA FILLETS
(OR ATLANTIC SALMON)
CUT IN 3cm CUBES**

8 FRESH ASPARAGUS SPEARS, HALVED

ABOUT 4 LARGE HANDFULS OF ROCKET

12 CHERRY TOMATOES, QUARTERED

1 LEBANESE CUCUMBER, SLICED

HEAT OIL IN NON-STICK PAN.

COOK FISH ON HIGH HEAT UNTIL BROWNED ON BOTH SIDES AND FLESH JUST FLAKES.

BOIL ASPARAGUS AND RINSE UNDER COLD WATER.

ARRANGE ROCKET, TOMATOES, ASPARAGUS AND CUCUMBER IN SERVING BOWL.

TOP WITH HOT FISH.

DRIZZLE WITH BALSAMIC DRESSING.

SERVE WITH CRUSTY BREAD.

BALSAMIC DRESSING:

80ml / 1/3 CUP BALSAMIC VINEGAR

2 TABLESPOONS LEMON OR LIME JUICE

2 TEASPOONS DIJON MUSTARD

FRESHLY GROUND BLACK PEPPER

2 TEASPOONS VIRGIN OLIVE OIL

COMBINE IN A SCREW-TOP CONTAINER AND SHAKE.

THIS IS NOT A GREENFISH,
AND IT'S NOT JUMPING.
BUT WHAT CAN YOU EXPECT
FROM AN IN-EXPENSIVE BOOK

PINK SEA RISING FISH STEW

SERVES 4.

¹/₂ CAPSICUM, FINELY CHOPPED

1 LARGE ONION, PEELED AND CHOPPED

1 TABLESPOON OLIVE OIL

1 MEDIUM CAN TOMATOES

2 TABLESPOONS CHOPPED PARSLEY

¹/₂ TEASPOON CAYENNE PEPPER

100g/4oz ZUCCHINI/COURGETTE

4 FILLETS OCEAN PERCH (OR SO) — CHOPPED IN 2cm CUBES

SALT AND PEPPER

SAUTE ONION LIGHTLY IN OLIVE OIL 2-3 MINUTES.

ADD TOMATOES, PARSLEY, CAPSICUM, CAYENNE AND SALT AND PEPPER.

STIR WELL, BRING TO BOIL AND COOK 2-3 MINUTES.

ADD ZUCCHINI AND FISH, RETURN TO BOIL, COVER AND SIMMER UNTIL FISH IS COOKED.

SERVE OVER RICE.

VARIATIONS ARE ENDLESS, JUST CHANGE THE VEGETABLES.

CYCLONE ERNIE FISH PARCELS

SERVES 4.

I was eating fish parcels on an island in the middle of Erakor Lagoon in Vanuatu which is like going back to 1950. Tomorrow they could shoot McHale's Navy there without building a set.

While most of the other resorts and towns in the Pacific have an architectural style called Crappola Moderne, Vanuatu has an award-winning style called Haven't Changed a Thing. Ten out of ten.

But the natives were looking nervous as lightning flashed over the horizon.

I had been listening to the radio for two days. There are two radio stations in Vanuatu. One is French spoken at machine-gun speed. The other is pidgin. The two radio stations come on air at random and apparently unannounced times.

I know only one phrase of pidgin. In English it says, What time big bird fall down out of sky? Which is the make-your-knees-shake version of, What time does the flight arrive?

Over two days I had discovered that there might be two cyclones nearby, in pidgin, French and Amazing Static.

One may have been a thousand kilometres to the east and the other a thousand kilometres to the west. Maybe.

The weather was bright but it was night. The surf on the outer reef was roaring like thousands of tigers.

The outdoor island cafe I was eating at was about six feet above sea level. But salt water was pouring into my shoes.

In the mess of Pidgin and French plus static, I thought that one of the cyclones was called Ernie. If I was right, Ernie was coming to get me.

So I drank heavily and slept similarly. In the morning the weather was perfect.

In memory of fish parcels and that fearful night I name this dish Cyclone Ernie.

4 OILY OR WHITE FISH CUTLETS
125ml/$^{1}/_{2}$ CUP COCONUT MILK
2 TABLESPOONS SOY SAUCE
2 CLOVES GARLIC, CHOPPED
2 RED CHILLIES, CHOPPED
40g/$^{1}/_{3}$ CUP SHALLOTS, CHOPPED
$^{1}/_{2}$ TEASPOON CUMIN
$^{1}/_{2}$ TEASPOON CORIANDER
$^{1}/_{4}$ TEASPOON TURMERIC

PREHEAT OVEN TO 200°C/400°F/GAS MARK 6.

COMBINE COCONUT MILK, SOY SAUCE, GARLIC, CHILLIES, SHALLOTS, CUMIN, CORIANDER AND TURMERIC.

MIX WELL.

PLACE 4 SHEETS OF FOIL ON BENCH, 1 FILLET ON EACH. RAISE SIDES OF FOIL.

POUR $1/4$ OF COCONUT MILK MIXTURE ON EACH.

FOLD FOIL TO ENCLOSE FISH AND JUICES, FORMING SMALL PARCELS.

BAKE FOR 10 MINUTES ON BAKING TRAY (OR UNTIL TENDER).

SERVE WITH STEAMED RICE.

PIDGIN

WARM DARWIN DAYS

TANGY FISH FILLETS

SERVES 4.

**4 200g/7oz FISH FILLETS
(HAKE OR SIMILAR)**
100g/$^1/_2$ CUP MAYONNAISE
1 TABLESPOON CAPERS
1 TABLESPOON PICKLED CUCUMBERS
1 TABLESPOON CORIANDER OR DILL
60g/$^1/_2$ CUP CHEDDAR CHEESE, GRATED
HANDFUL OF FRESH BREADCRUMBS
2 DESSERTSPOONS BUTTER
LEMON OR ORANGE ZEST TO GARNISH

PAT FISH FILLETS DRY. PLACE INTO FOIL-LINED GRILL PAN.

SEASON WITH SALT AND FRESHLY GROUND
BLACK PEPPER.

IN A BOWL, COMBINE MAYONNAISE, CAPERS,
PICKLED CUCUMBERS AND CORIANDER AND SPREAD
OVER THE FILLETS.

IN ANOTHER BOWL, COMBINE CHEESE AND
BREADCRUMBS. SPRINKLE OVER FILLETS, DOT WITH
BUTTER AND SEASON.

GRILL UNTIL GOLDEN AND CRISPY — ABOUT 10
MINUTES, DEPENDING ON THICKNESS.

GARNISH WITH LEMON OR ORANGE ZEST AND SERVE
WITH SALAD AND RICE, OR MAYBE BAKED POTATOES.

BLUE PACIFIC NOON GRILLED ATLANTIC SALMON CUTLETS

SERVES 6.

SPLASH OF DRY VERMOUTH

6 ATLANTIC SALMON CUTLETS

4 TABLESPOONS BUTTER, MELTED

1 TEASPOON FRESH LEMON THYME

1 TEASPOON PEPPER

1 LEMON, THINLY SLICED

LEMON THYME FOR GARNISH

BRUSH FISH WITH MELTED BUTTER ON BAKING DISH.

SPRINKLE WITH LEMON THYME AND SEASON.

ARRANGE LEMON SLICES ON TOP, SPLASH WITH VERMOUTH.

WRAP FOIL LOOSELY AROUND THE FISH.

GRILL FOR 10-15 MINUTES OR UNTIL FISH FLAKES WHEN TOUCHED WITH FORK.

REMOVE FOIL.

GARNISH WITH LEMON THYME.

SERVE WITH SEASONAL VEGETABLES.

BUTTERNUT BLUE CRISP PRAWN SALAD

SERVES 6.

1 BUTTERNUT PUMPKIN, PEELED

3 MEDIUM BEETROOTS, PEELED

2 SWEET POTATOES, PEELED

**30 PRAWNS, SHELLED, DEVEINED
  AND CLEANED**

OIL FOR FRYING

MARINADE:

**1 TEASPOON ROOT GINGER,
  FINELY GRATED**

2 TABLESPOONS TOASTED SESAME OIL

3 TEASPOONS OYSTER SAUCE

3 TEASPOONS SOY SAUCE

60ml/$\frac{1}{4}$ CUP ORANGE JUICE

SLICE THE BUTTERNUT, BEETROOT AND SWEET
POTATO INTO 1cm SLICES.

MIX GINGER WITH 15ml OF SESAME OIL,
SOY SAUCE, OYSTER SAUCE AND ORANGE JUICE.

MARINATE PRAWNS FOR 30 MINUTES.

HEAT OIL IN DEEP PAN. FRY BUTTERNUT, BEETROOT
AND SWEET POTATO SLICES SEPARATELY IN BATCHES

UNTIL CRISP.

DRAIN ON ABSORBENT PAPER.

HEAT REMAINING SESAME OIL AND FRY PRAWNS,
POUR IN THE MARINADE AND BRING TO THE BOIL.

ARRANGE BUTTERNUT, BEETROOT AND SWEET POTATO
CHIPS ONTO SERVING PLATES.

SPOON 5 PRAWNS PER SERVING AND A LITTLE
MARINADE OVER THE CHIPS.

SERVE IMMEDIATELY WITH SALAD.

VARIATION: TRY PARSNIP CHIPS.

MANGO MANGO SMOKED SALMON, AVOCADO AND MANGO SALAD

SERVES 4.

1 AVOCADO, CUT INTO SLICES

16 SLICES SMOKED SALMON

1 MANGO, CUT INTO STRIPS

75g/$\frac{1}{2}$ CUP CROUTONS

60g/$\frac{1}{2}$ CUP WALNUTS, HALVED

ASSORTED SALAD LEAVES, WASHED

ARRANGE LETTUCE LEAVES ON INDIVIDUAL PLATES.

ARRANGE SALMON, AVOCADO AND MANGO ON TOP.

GARNISH WITH CROUTONS AND WALNUTS.

POUR DILL MAYONNAISE OVER.

DILL MAYONNAISE:

2 TABLESPOONS WHITE WINE VINEGAR

1 TEASPOON CASTOR SUGAR

1 TEASPOON SEED MUSTARD

4 TABLESPOONS OLIVE OIL

1 TEASPOON DILL, CHOPPED

PINCH OF SALT

WHISK TOGETHER VINEGAR, SALT AND SUGAR
UNTIL DISSOLVED.

SLOWLY WHISK IN MUSTARD AND OLIVE OIL
UNTIL WELL MIXED.

ADD THE DILL AND POUR OVER SALAD.

Post-modern mango

FREE CHILLI STEAMED FISH

SERVES 4.

I was in a cell with Pablo Neruda in the dark days of revolution.

He wrote beautiful poems on the dim cream walls with charcoal from an open fire that was never lit.

Sixty days and sixty nights. Then the sound of gunshots in the streets. The sound of running footsteps down the stone corridors.

Would they bring freedom...or would they bring a bullet? They brought neither.

They brought steamed fish with chilli and fragrant herbs. And they brought freedom. All I can bring you is the recipe.

Unexpected howling dog

**800g/1³/₄lb SNAPPER,
IN BITE-SIZE PIECES**

2 TABLESPOONS VEGETABLE OIL

2 TABLESPOONS CHOPPED GARLIC

250ml/1 CUP LIME JUICE

6 TABLESPOONS THAI FISH SAUCE

PINCH OF SUGAR

**2 TABLESPOONS EACH OF CHOPPED
CORIANDER, BASIL, GINGER,
LEMON GRASS, SPRING ONIONS**

**8 FRESH KAFFIR LIME LEAVES,
ROUGHLY CHOPPED**

2 TABLESPOONS CHOPPED RED CHILLIES

MARINATE SNAPPER IN OIL AND 1 TABLESPOON
OF THAI FISH SAUCE FOR 10 MINUTES.

STEAM FISH UNTIL COOKED.

COMBINE ALL OTHER INGREDIENTS IN A BOWL.

ARRANGE FISH ON PLATTER.

POUR OVER SAUCE AND SERVE.

CHINATOWN CUTLETS ORIENTAL TUNA

SERVES 4.

4 TUNA CUTLETS

60ml/$\frac{1}{4}$ CUP FRESH ORANGE JUICE

60ml/$\frac{1}{4}$ CUP SOY SAUCE

60ml/$\frac{1}{4}$ CUP OYSTER SAUCE

2 TABLESPOONS CHOPPED PARSLEY

1 TABLESPOON LEMON JUICE

1 TEASPOON GRATED LEMON RIND

1 CLOVE OF GARLIC, CRUSHED

1 TEASPOON GARAM MASALA

COMBINE ALL INGREDIENTS IN A SHALLOW DISH.

MARINATE TUNA CUTLETS IN THIS MIXTURE
FOR THREE HOURS.

GRILL CUTLETS FOR ABOUT 3 MINUTES EACH SIDE,
BASTING WITH MARINADE DURING COOKING.

SERVE WITH GREEN SALAD TOSSED IN LEMON JUICE
AND HONEY.

PRINCESS'S TAKEAWAY SALMON AND CAVIAR PIZZA

SERVES 2.

LOGOS BEGAN WHEN MURDEROUS THUGS IN DISTANT CENTURIES BECAME SUCCESSFUL ENOUGH TO HAVE PERSONAL LOGOS WHICH WERE THEN CALLED HERALDRY. HERALDRY CAUSED CONSIDERABLE EXCITEMENT AND QUICKLY LEAD TO PAGEANTRY.

PAGEANTRY WAS BASED ON THE ABILITY TO RUN POPULAR EVENTS AND HAVE YOUR LOGO HELD ALOFT ON BIG STICKS.

OVER THE YEARS, WITH THE HELP OF HERALDRY AND PAGEANTRY, THE DESCENDANTS OF THE MOST SUCCESSFUL OF THE PSYCHOPATHS BECAME KNOWN AS ROYALTY.

THIS THEN LED TO THE ESTABLISHMENT OF CORPORATE HEADQUARTERS WHICH WERE KNOWN AS PALACES.

IF THE PALACES WERE USING TOTAL QUALITY MANAGEMENT THEN THE MEALS WERE SERVED ON TIME AND THE HORSES WERE GROOMED PROPERLY. ALL OF THIS MEANT THAT THE PALACES OF ROYALTY GREW LARGER AS THE CHINS OF ROYALTY GREW SMALLER.

BUT WHAT OF THE POOR PEOPLE WHO DIDN'T HAVE LOGOS? WELL, THEY DID IN A SENSE. IN RETURN FOR OBEDIENCE THEY WERE GRANTED ILLITERACY.

Through illiteracy they got logos, given to them so that trade could become simpler.

The poor people drank beer and ate pizzas.

If the publican painted the word 'BEER' on his sign it didn't mean much to them because they couldn't read. For all they knew it might say, Enrol here for a life in the army.

It just wasn't worth taking the risk.

But if the publican painted a big foaming jug of beer on his sign he's got you. He's got me, anyway. Welcome to the poor people's first logo.

The same applied to takeaway food. So to make up for all the crap food you ate in the 13th Century here's a pizza fit for a princess.

Is any of this making sense?

No wonder Billy Joe Macallister jumped off the Tallahassee Bridge.

2 VERY THIN, COOKED PIZZA BASES

125ml/$\frac{1}{2}$ CUP FRESH TOMATO SAUCE (OR USE TOMATO PUREE)

80ml/$\frac{1}{3}$ CUP SOUR CREAM

200g/7oz SMOKED SALMON

4 TABLESPOONS CAVIAR

1 TABLESPOON CHOPPED DILL

SPREAD TOMATO SAUCE OVER BASES.

COVER WITH SOUR CREAM.

LAYER THE SMOKED SALMON OVER THE CREAM.

SPREAD CAVIAR ON TOP.

COOK AT 200°C/400°F/GAS MARK 6 UNTIL HOT
(ABOUT 10 MINUTES), SPRINKLE WITH CHOPPED DILL.

SERVE WITH A GREEN SALAD.

THURSDAY'S BREAKFAST
STEAMED CRAB

This is not a lie.

Once upon a time I was marooned at a beach during a huge storm.

I had driven 40km down a fire trail in an old Volkswagen. In the same few hours I arrived at the beach, my battery went flat and the hinterland behind the beach became flooded. I was stranded for forty days and never saw a human being.

I had no fishing lines but I did have underwater goggles. About 100 metres off the beach was a reef. It was covered in lobsters. I could swim out and grab one in each hand and lie on my back and kick my way to the beach. The lobsters then made clicking noises that I believe sharks are pleased to hear.

Behind the beach were groves of banana trees. I cooked the lobster in my Volkswagen's hub caps. Then I had lobster and banana day after day, meal after meal. One day I caught a crab that was so gigantic, I thought that it might maim me. But I won the battle and ate it for breakfast. Crab and bananas.
I think it was a Thursday.

1 LEMON, SLICED

500ml/2 CUPS WATER

500ml/2 CUPS WHITE VINEGAR

FRESH CRABS (1 PER PERSON, DEPENDS ON SIZE)

1 TABLESPOON DRY MUSTARD

1 TEASPOON PAPRIKA

PUT WATER, WHITE VINEGAR AND SLICED LEMON INTO BASE OF STEAMER.

SPRINKLE CRABS WITH MUSTARD AND PAPRIKA AND PLACE IN TOP HALF OF STEAMER.

CLOSE TIGHTLY AND STEAM OVER MODERATE HEAT UNTIL COOKED (ABOUT 15 MINUTES, DEPENDING ON SIZE).

WARATAH STREET HIDEOUT

TUNA AND SPAGHETTI

SPAGHETTI

CANS OF TUNA, ONE VERY SMALL CAN PER PERSON

SEVERAL CLOVES OF GARLIC

BUTTER

CHOPPED PARSLEY

SLICE GARLIC CLOVES UP INTO SMALL PIECES.

PUT SOME BUTTER INTO A PAN AND FOLLOW WITH GARLIC AND CHOPPED PARSLEY.

TOAST IT AS BROWN OR BLACK AS YOU LIKE.

PUT SPAGHETTI INTO BOILING WATER.

WHEN COOKED, DRAIN.

SERVE SPAGHETTI INTO INDIVIDUAL BOWLS.

PUT TUNA ON TOP OF SPAGHETTI.

POUR GARLIC MIX ON TOP OF TUNA AND SPAGHETTI.

SERVE WITH A SIMPLE SIDE SALAD.

MANGO WATERFALL

REDFISH WITH MANGO

SERVES 4.

4 REDFISH FILLETS

125ml/½ CUP DRY WHITE WINE

½ TEASPOON GROUND BAY LEAVES

1 MANGO, PEELED AND SLICED

660g/4 CUPS HOT,
  COOKED LONG-GRAIN RICE

POACH FILLETS IN WINE UNTIL THEY FLAKE WHEN TOUCHED WITH FORK.

REMOVE TO SERVING PLATTER AND KEEP WARM.

ADD BAY LEAVES AND MANGO TO WINE.

SIMMER 3 MINUTES, REMOVE BAY LEAVES.

ARRANGE MANGO ON TOP OF THE FISH.

POUR SAUCE OVER.

SERVE WITH RICE.

RED BUTTERFLY MUSTARD PRAWNS

SERVES 4.

**1kg/2lb LARGE GREEN PRAWNS,
GUTTED, CLEANED AND HEADED**

150g/5oz BUTTER

1 TABLESPOON OLIVE OIL

1 TABLESPOON FINELY CHOPPED ONION

$^1/_2$ TEASPOON CHOPPED GARLIC

1 TEASPOON DIJON MUSTARD

**1 TEASPOON CHOPPED FRESH HERBS
(TARRAGON OR PARSLEY)**

125ml/$^1/_2$ CUP BRANDY

125ml/$^1/_2$ CUP CREAM

FRESHLY GROUND BLACK PEPPER

SALT IF NEEDED

CUT CLEANED PRAWNS DOWN CENTRE AND
OPEN OUT BUTTERFLY-STYLE, LEAVING TAIL INTACT.

MELT HALF THE BUTTER IN DEEP PAN.

ADD PRAWNS, ONION, GARLIC, MUSTARD,
HERBS, PEPPER AND SALT.

COOK OVER MEDIUM HEAT FOR 8-10 MINUTES, ACCORDING TO SIZE OF PRAWNS.

ADD BRANDY TO PAN. THEN FLAME.

ADD CREAM, THEN THICKEN WITH REMAINING BUTTER.

SERVE ON HOT PLATES IMMEDIATELY WITH SALAD AND WILD RICE.

COOK IT AGAIN SAM MOROCCAN FISH

SERVES 4-6.

I was in Morocco once. Loved it.

Very, very exciting place if you didn't stay at the Hilton.

A fine place to drink four blocks back from the tourists.

But when they stamped my passport on the way out, I felt very relieved that I hadn't offended anyone in some of the bars five blocks back.

6 JEWFISH CUTLETS

2 ONIONS, SLICED

5 TABLESPOONS OLIVE OIL

250ml/1 CUP TOMATO PASTE

6 OLIVES (OR SO)

1 TABLESPOON CHOPPED PARSLEY

SALT AND PEPPER

FRESH CHOPPED CORIANDER

PUT SLICED ONIONS ONTO HEATPROOF DISH, TOP WITH FRESH CORIANDER.

PLACE FISH FILLETS ON TOP.

ADD OIL AND TOMATO PASTE AND POUR WATER OVER FISH UNTIL IT IS JUST COVERED.

ADD OLIVES, PARSLEY, SALT AND PEPPER.

BAKE IN MODERATE OVEN FOR 45 MINUTES.

SERVE WITH COUSCOUS AND GREEN SALAD.

THIS AEROPLANE IS AN OBSCURE REFERENCE TO THE LAST SCENE IN CASABLANCA

JAMAICA RAFT CREOLE FILLETS

SERVES 6.

3 TABLESPOONS OLIVE OIL

2 MEDIUM ONIONS, PEELED AND SLICED

1 GREEN PEPPER, SEEDED AND SLICED

1 RED PEPPER, SEEDED AND SLICED

1 STALK OF CELERY, CHOPPED

**1/2 TEASPOON CHILLI POWDER
   (OR TO TASTE)**

SALT

FRESHLY GROUND BLACK PEPPER

1kg/2lb WHITE FISH FILLETS, CUBED

**1 410g/14oz CAN WHOLE TOMATOES,
   CHOPPED**

2 TABLESPOONS TOMATO PUREE

1 DESSERTSPOON BROWN SUGAR

SAUTE ONIONS, GREEN AND RED PEPPERS
AND CELERY UNTIL TENDER.

ADD CHILLI POWDER, SALT, PEPPER AND FISH.

STIR MIXTURE TOGETHER.

POUR TOMATO, TOMATO PUREE AND SUGAR
INTO THE SAUCEPAN.

SIMMER GENTLY UNTIL THE FISH IS COOKED THROUGH.

SERVE WITH RICE.

JAILHOUSE FILLET DORY FILLETS WITH AVOCADO MACADAMIA CREAM

SERVES 4.

- **1 RIPE AVOCADO, PEELED, SEEDED AND CUT INTO CHUNKS**
- **30g/$^1/_4$ CUP ROASTED MACADAMIA NUTS, SKINNED**
- **125g/$^1/_2$ CUP SOFT CREAM CHEESE**
- **2 TABLESPOONS LEMON JUICE**
- **2 TABLESPOONS BUTTER**

MIX AVOCADO, MACADAMIA NUTS, CREAM CHEESE AND LEMON JUICE IN BLENDER UNTIL SMOOTH.

MELT BUTTER IN FRYING PAN.

PUT SEVERAL DORY FILLETS IN PAN AT A TIME.

COVER WITH AVOCADO CREAM.

GENTLY POACH FOR 6-8 MINUTES OR UNTIL FLESH FLAKES.

SERVE WITH BOILED NEW POTATOES AND GREEN BEANS.

SLARKI YARKI TERIYAKI KINGFISH

SERVES 2.

2 KINGFISH FILLETS
1 TEASPOON FRESH GRATED GINGER
1 TABLESPOON SOY SAUCE
1 TABLESPOON MIRIN (RICE VINEGAR) OR SWEET SHERRY
LEMON JUICE OR FRESHLY GRATED HORSERADISH

MARINATE WHOLE FILLETS IN SOY SAUCE, MIRIN AND GINGER FOR 1-2 HOURS.

THREAD EACH FILLET ONTO TWO PARALLEL SKEWERS TO KEEP IT FIRM AND GRILL UNTIL COOKED. (SOAK SKEWERS IN COLD WATER FIRST TO PREVENT THEM FROM BURNING.)

SERVE WITH LEMON JUICE OR HORSERADISH.

ET TU BANANA BANANA OR MANGO FILLETS

SERVES 4-6.

4-6 FILLETS OF WHITE FISH (LING, FLAKE, OCEAN PERCH)

1 CAN COCONUT MILK

2 BANANAS, SLICED

OR

2 MANGOES, SLICED

1 TEASPOON CURRY POWDER

1/2 TEASPOON CUMIN

FRESHLY GROUND BLACK PEPPER

1/2 TEASPOON GARAM MASALA

PUT LAYERS OF FISH AND FRUIT IN OVENPROOF DISH.

MIX SPICES WITH COCONUT MILK.

POUR OVER FISH AND FRUIT.

BAKE AT 180°C/350°F/GAS MARK 4 FOR 30 MINUTES.

SERVE WITH GREEN SALAD AND BAKED POTATOES.

YELLOW BUTTERFLY PASTA WITH SALMON

SERVES 3-4.

1 200g/7oz CAN SALMON IN OIL
400g/14oz PASTA
   (VARY THE TYPE YOU USE)
150g/5oz MUSHROOMS
1 CLOVE GARLIC, CHOPPED
1 TEASPOON CAPERS, CHOPPED
1 TOMATO, DICED
60ml/$^1/_4$ CUP DRY WHITE WINE
FRESHLY GROUND BLACK PEPPER
1 TABLESPOON GRATED
   PARMESAN CHEESE

STRAIN SALMON AND SAVE OIL.

BOIL LARGE POT OF SALTED WATER AND COOK PASTA.

SLICE WASHED MUSHROOMS.

HEAT SALMON OIL IN SAUCEPAN AND GENTLY FRY GARLIC AND CAPERS FOR A FEW SECONDS.

ADD MUSHROOMS. STIR-FRY FOR A MINUTE.

ADD TOMATO AND COOK 3-4 MINUTES, ADD WINE.

CRUMBLE SALMON INTO PAN AND SEASON.

POUR OVER PASTA AND MIX THROUGH.

SPRINKLE WITH PARMESAN CHEESE AND PEPPER AND SERVE.

IT'S A LUNCH OR A SIMPLE SUPPER.

SOUGHING SEA CEVICHE

SERVES 4-6.

500g/1lb FIRM WHITE FISH FILLETS (SNAPPER, DORY, BREAM)

1 TEASPOON SALT

60ml/¼ CUP LEMON OR LIME JUICE

1 MEDIUM ONION, FINELY CHOPPED

60ml/¼ CUP COCONUT MILK

1 GREEN PEPPER, FINELY CHOPPED IN SLIVERS

6 CHERRY TOMATOES, HALVED

1 CHILLI, SLICED, SEEDED

CUT FISH INTO BITE-SIZE PIECES.

SPRINKLE WITH SALT, LEMON JUICE AND CHILLI.

COVER AND CHILL FOR 2 HOURS OR UNTIL FISH WHITENS, STIRRING OCCASIONALLY.

DRAIN.

STIR IN ONION, GREEN PEPPER AND COCONUT MILK.

PUT TOMATOES ON TOP.

SERVE CHILLED.

A GREAT SUMMER ENTREE OR ACCOMPANIMENT TO SALADS.

COOKING FISH

POACHING

JUST COVER THE FISH IN LIQUID (WATER AND/OR WINE, STOCK, MILK, BEER, VINEGAR, LEMON JUICE).

ADD ONION, PEPPERCORNS, A BAY LEAF.

COOK GENTLY BELOW BOILING POINT, 8-15 MINUTES, DEPENDING ON SIZE.

LEAVE IN POACHING LIQUID IF DISH IS TO BE SERVED COLD, SO IT STAYS MOIST.

GOOD FOR LING, SNAPPER, PERCH, WHOLE WHITING, DORY, CORAL TROUT.

BAKING

IF WHOLE, YOU MAY WISH TO STUFF IT FIRST (TRY COOKED RICE, GRATED LEMON RIND AND SAUTEED MUSHROOMS).

GREASE BAKING DISH AND PUT FISH IN.

ADD SEASONING AND LIQUID (TOMATO OR LEMON JUICE, WINE, HONEY AND SOY ETC).

BRUSH FISH WITH OIL, PEPPER AND SALT.

COVER DISH ROUGHLY WITH FOIL AND BAKE AT 180°/350°F/GAS MARK 4 UNTIL DONE (TIME DEPENDS ON SIZE).

PAN FRYING

GOOD FOR SMALL FILLETS (WHITING, DORY, SILVER BREAM).

USE A MIXTURE OF OIL AND BUTTER, OR GHEE.

COOK 3-5 MINUTES ACCORDING TO SIZE, UNTIL GOLDEN AND FLAKY.

STEAMING

USE FIRM MOIST FISH LIKE SNAPPER,
GEMFISH, LING.

STEAM OVER BOILING
WATER UNTIL FLESH FLAKES.

MAY BE WRAPPED IN FOIL.

GRILLING

BRUSH FISH WITH MELTED BUTTER,
LEMON JUICE OR WHITE WINE
(TO PREVENT DRYING OUT).

SCORE THICK FISH DIAGONALLY 2 OR 3
TIMES ON OUTER SKIN FOR EVEN COOKING.

PLACE UNDER HEATED GRILL
(ON MODERATE HEAT).

BASTE **AGAIN** DURING COOKING,
AND TURN ONCE.

GOOD FOR MULLET, TAILOR,
LING, PERCH, SOLE, BREAM.

BARBECUING

ALLOW FIRE TO BURN DOWN TO EMBERS (NO FLAMES).

BRUSH BARBECUE GRILL WITH OIL FIRST.

BASTE FISH WITH OIL, OR OIL AND BUTTER MIX, OR LEMON JUICE (OR BE INVENTIVE).

OR **WRAP** IN FOIL.

WHOLE FISH OR FILLETS, THEY CAN ALL BE BARBECUED.

ALWAYS READ **ALL THE RECIPE** BEFORE YOU START.
ALWAYS MAKE SURE YOU HAVE **ALL THE INGREDIENTS** BEFORE YOU START.

FISH & CRUSTACEAN IDENTIFICATION

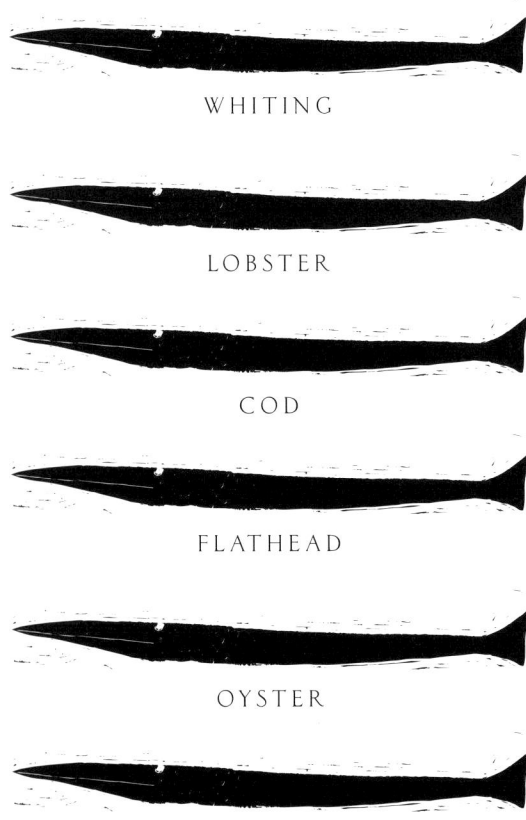

WHITING

LOBSTER

COD

FLATHEAD

OYSTER

BLUE SWIMMER CRAB

Fish & Crustacean Identification

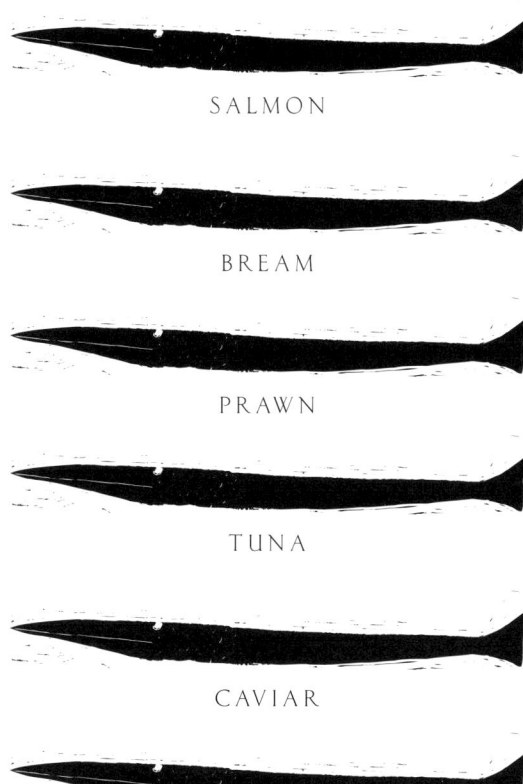

SALMON

BREAM

PRAWN

TUNA

CAVIAR

REDFISH

Fish & Crustacean Identification

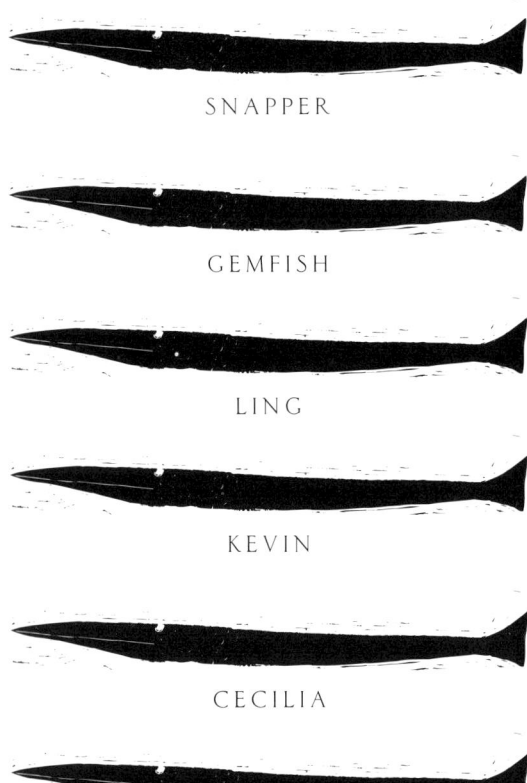

SNAPPER

GEMFISH

LING

KEVIN

CECILIA

MULLET

Fish & Crustacean Identification

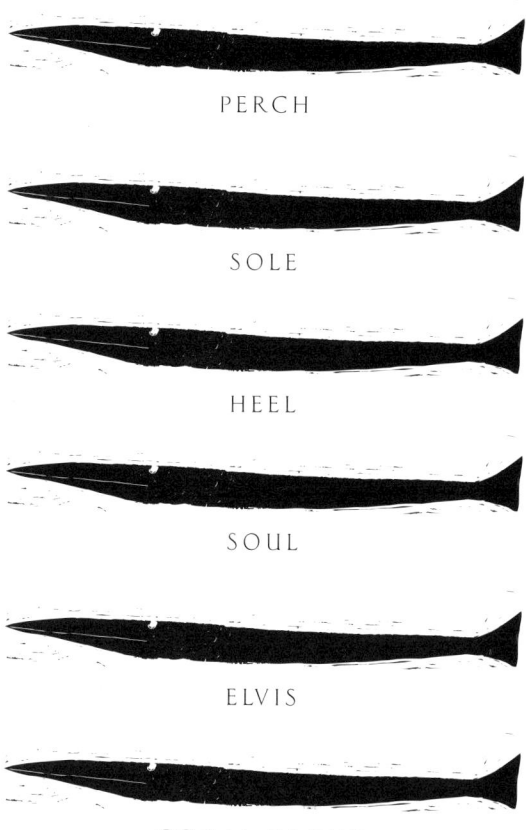

PERCH

SOLE

HEEL

SOUL

ELVIS

CORAL TROUT

OTHER BOOKS IN THE ZIGGY ZEN SERIES:

A cookbook for a man who
probably only owns one saucepan

ISBN: 1902813146

The mafia just moved in next door and
they're dropping by for dinner cookbook

ISBN: 1902813154

How to become a dinner party legend and
avoid crippling psychological damage

ISBN: 1902813162

For more titles, visit
Lagoon Books website at
www.lagoongames.com